History

Cities, Castles, Churches –
The Middle Ages

D1718451

Umschlagbild: Buchmalerei aus dem 12. Jahrhundert. Abgebildet sind Zisterziensermönche bei der Verrichtung ihrer täglichen Arbeit.

1. Auflage

1 ^{5 4 3 2 1} | 15 14 13 12 11

5 4 3 2 1 | 15 14 13 12 11

Alle Drucke dieser Auflage sind unverändert und können im Unterricht nebeneinander verwendet werden.
Die letzte Zahl bezeichnet das Jahr des Druckes.

Autorinnen und Autoren: Dr. Christine Tiefenthal (S. 8–19, S. 52–63), Martin Wicke (S. 20–43), Heike Kremer (S. 44–51)

Redaktion: Beate Klemm, Leipzig
Herstellung: Kerstin Heisch
Bildassistenz: Katja Schnürpel

Illustrationen: Sandy Lohß, Chemnitz
Kartografien: Ingenieurbüro für Kartografie J. Zwick, Gießen
Satz: Anne Lehmann, Leipzig
Reproduktion: Meyle+Müller GmbH+Co. KG, Pforzheim
Druck: Mediahaus Biering GmbH, München

Printed in Germany
ISBN 978-3-12-460082-0

9 783124 600820

History

Cities, Castles, Churches – The Middle Ages

Heike Kremer
Dr. Christine Tiefenthal
Martin Wicke

Ernst Klett Verlag
Stuttgart · Leipzig

Online-Link
460082-0005
Glossary of Key Terms

So arbeitest du mit dem Heft

Das Heft ist in vier Module unterteilt. Jedes dieser Module behandelt ein Thema, z. B. Ritter und Burgen im Mittelalter.

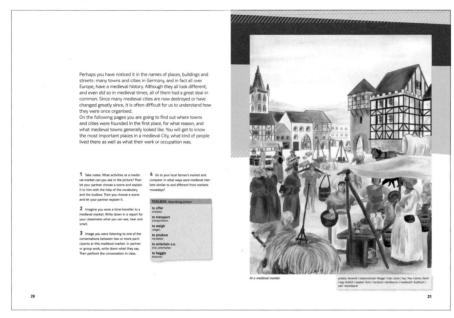

Die Auftaktdoppelseiten am Beginn jedes Moduls bieten dir mit Informationen und Aufgaben einen Einstieg in das jeweilige Thema.

Überschriften markieren die Kapitel.
Deine Lehrerin oder dein Lehrer kann aussuchen, welche Kapitel ihr im Unterricht behandelt.

Quellentexte stehen auf gelbem Untergrund. Diese wurden entweder in der Vergangenheit geschrieben oder sind von Historikerinnen und Historikern über die Vergangenheit verfasst worden.

Wenn du die nummerierten Aufgaben bearbeitet hast, bist du ein Experte für das Thema des Moduls.

Die sogenannten Verfassertexte haben wir, die Autorinnen des Heftes, geschrieben.

Auf www.klett.de kannst du die angegebene Ziffernfolge des Online-Links eintippen. Du wirst dann auf interessante Webseiten geleitet oder erhältst zusätzliches Material.

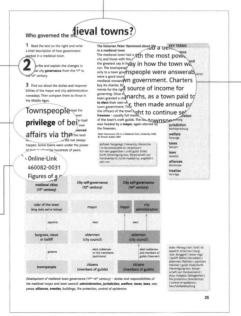

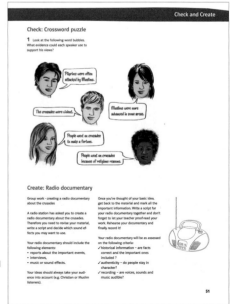

Auf der „Check and Create"-Seite kannst du dein Wissen überprüfen und ein Produkt zum Abschluss des Moduls erstellen.

Vokabelhilfen

Das „How to"-Vokabular unterstützt dich darin, über Textquellen, Bilder, Statistiken und anderes mehr auf Englisch zu sprechen.

Du findest es auf zwei Seiten, nämlich im vorderen und im hinteren Umschlag.

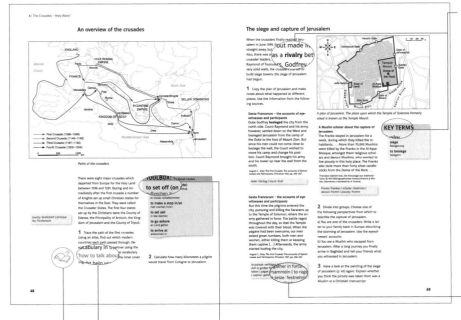

In einigen Texten stehen fett gedruckte Wörter. Das sind „Key Terms" (Schlüsselbegriffe), die in der Randspalte übersetzt werden.

Diese wichtigen Begriffe solltest du auf Englisch und Deutsch auswendig lernen. Eine Zusammenstellung aller „Key Terms" des Heftes findest du auf www.klett.de unter der Nummer 460082-0005.

In Vokabelkästen unter Texten werden die Wörter aus dem Text übersetzt, die du vielleicht noch nicht kennst.

Diese Wörter dienen dem Textverständnis. Du musst sie nicht auswendig lernen.

Blau markierte Wörter und ein blaues Symbol in der Randspalte verweisen auf das „How to"-Vokabular.

Die Richtung des Pfeils zeigt dir, ob du nach vorne oder hinten blättern musst.

In den „Toolboxes" (Werkzeugkästen) werden dir englische Wendungen vorgestellt.

In bestimmten Aufgaben wirst du aufgefordert, eine „Toolbox" zu benutzen.

1 Living in a village in the Middle Ages

90 to 95 percent of all medieval people lived in the countryside in villages. A medieval village consisted of more than a dozen farmsteads. Most of the land was owned by the lord. The lord's house and his land were called the manor.

The manor and the village or settlements around it were the central unit for rural life in the Middle Ages, the center of life for the people in the countryside.

Find out about life in a medieval village: Who lived in a village? What were the houses like? How was the work organized and how was food produced?

1 Copy the village plan (p. 9) into your history folder and fill in the words above the plan in the right positions.

2 Take a look at the picture and imagine: Who lived there, what did people eat, what jobs did they have? Talk about your ideas in class.

3 Walking around a medieval village: Act out the plan of the village. See the activity box for help.

4 Choose one person in the picture. Now draw a speech bubble into your history folder. Write into it what the person thinks.

ACTIVITY BOX: Acting out a village plan

Use the classroom space, that means:

1 Stack tables and chairs.

2 Walk about and position yourself e.g. as the church, a house, a pig, a tree, a peasant, a field, ...
Mime what or who you are or write it on a piece of paper to show the others.

3 One half of your class acts the village, the others walk around it. Then swop.

There were peasants' cottages, a church, a manor, fields, common land, meadows, a forest, a river, a water mill …

This is what a medieval village might have looked like.

to stack: stapeln | mime: nachahmen | to swop: tauschen | manor: Herrenhaus/Herrensitz/Landgut | rural: ländlich | peasant: Bauer | cottage: Häuschen/Hütte | meadow: Wiese | farmstead: Bauernhof/Gehöft | common land: Gemeindeland, Allmende | Gemüsebeet: vegetable patch | half-timbered construction: Fachwerk | church: Kirche | roof: Dach | fence: Zaun | barrel: Fass | wood: Holz | corral: Pferch | barn: Scheune

Who lived in a medieval village?

KEY TERMS

peasant
Bauer

craftspeople
Handwerker

cottagers
Häuschenbewohner; jemand
der in einem Häuschen wohnt

villein
abhängiger Bauer/Leibeigener

freeman
freier Bauer

to protect
beschützen

prosperity
Reichtum

manor
Herrenhaus, Landgut

fine
Strafe, Bußgeld

to inherit
erben

property
Besitz

starvation
Hungertod/das Verhungern

After having taken a brief look at a medieval village, let us find out who lived there. In all villages you would find mostly **peasant** families, some **craftspeople**, a lord, and oftentimes a priest. **Cottagers** were divided into **villeins** and **freemen**, those who had to pay services to the lord on his estate and those who did not. The priest was a significant person because the Christian religion and religious rituals and practices were important in people's everyday life.

1 Read the texts and take a look at the pictures. Match the short texts and the pictures.

2 Get together with a partner. Look at the four pictures and choose one person each. Invent a dialogue. You could also work in groups of four and present the conversation.

A villein
Poor people spent all their lives working and producing food. Villeins had few rights, and worked their own and the lord's land. The lord was meant to **protect** them.

The lord
A lord was born a lord. The title and the **property** were **inherited**. He was interested in ensuring continuity on his land. His **prosperity** depended on motivated peasants. He lived in a **manor**. The peasants paid **fines** when they wanted to marry people outside his manor, when they inherited their father's land or wanted to travel abroad.

A freeman
A freeman had no duties except for paying a rent to the lord for the land. This person could move and live as he wanted to.
Not everybody could become a freeman. Usually, villeins stayed villeins, but some had the chance to become free, e.g. when the lord wanted them to be free or when a third person paid for their freedom.

A woman
Women played an important role in agricultural life. They worked in the fields and managed the household. Preserving and storing food was the basic responsibility of women and children. It was a hard life, especially when **starvation** was a real danger in many years.

everyday: Alltag | duty: Pflicht | rent: Miete | freedom: Freiheit | responsibility: Verantwortung

Visiting a peasant family in a cruck house

Peasants lived in cottages called cruck houses. The walls had a wooden frame (cruck) onto which wattle and daub was plastered. This was a mixture of mud, straw and manure. The roofs were thatched. Most of these cottages had only one room, about 5 x 3.5 m in size. They were of poor quality, not built to last. After some years the wood rotted and the building collapsed. This is why we do not have many houses of this kind from the medieval period.

Inside, the cottages in a medieval village were full of smoke because they did not have a chimney. Straw lined the mud floor. The houses were very hot in summer and very cold in winter. Windows were just holes in the walls. Doors were covered with a curtain as a wooden door was expensive. At night animals were brought inside in order to be safe. The houses had no running water, no toilets, no baths or wash basins. Soap and shampoo were not used. People were covered with dirt, fleas and lice. Beds were stuffed with straw.

1 Make a chart to compare your house or apartment and a medieval cruck house.

Comparing		
	medieval cottage	your home
toilets	No	Yes?
pigs	Yes	No?
heating	…	…
rooms	…	…
…	…	…

2 After reading the texts write a short newspaper article: Living in a medieval cruck house. Mention how people lived, what you could see. Don't forget about the Ws: where, when, who, how.

wattle and daub: Flechtwerk mit Lehmverstrich | mud: Lehm | straw: Stroh | manure: Mist | thatched: Reet gedeckt | smoke: Rauch | chimney: Schornstein | curtain: Vorhang | wash basin: Waschbecken | dirt: Schmutz | fleas: Flöhe | lice: Läuse

Living in a medieval cruck house.

bucket: Eimer | straw mattress: Strohsack | bedding: Schlafstelle | fireplace: Feuerstelle | to lie: liegen

Peasant life in feudalism

In a feudal society every person who held land **received protection** from their **superiors** but had to pay **duties** and services in return. Everybody knew his or her place in this social system which is called **feudalism**.

The king – at the top of the order of society – **let** land to the barons, the barons let land to knights, freemen or nobles, and all of them let land to peasants. The lords and nobles swore an **oath** to the king. They had to go to war when the king told them to do so or send a number of men.

Churchmen were at the same level as lords. The peasants were at the bottom of the feudal system which meant that they had to obey their lord, to whom they had sworn an **oath of obedience**. The villeins had to work on the fields of their masters: plough, **harvest** the corn, gather it in barns, and thresh and winnow the grain; they also had to mow and carry home the hay, cut and collect wood, tend the animals, pay rent for their land. 60% of the peasants were owned by the lord, who could sell them and make them work on his land whenever he needed them. A free peasant only had to work for a set number of days. A **tithe**, a **tax** to the church, was 10% of what the peasant had produced in a year. Peasants also had to work without payment on church land. No one broke this rule because the villeins believed that God would see their sins and **punish** them.

Adapted from: Chris Trueman: http://www.historylearningsite.co.uk/medieval_peasants.htm

obey: gehorchen | barn: Scheune | mow: mähen | hay: Heu | to sell: verkaufen | a set number: eine bestimmte Anzahl | sin: Sünde

KEY TERMS

to receive
erhalten

protection
Schutz

superiors
Höherstehende

duties
Pflichten

feudalism
Feudalismus, Herrschaftssystem

to let
leihen

oath
Eid

oath of obedience
Gehorsamseid

harvest
ernten

tithe
Zehnt

tax
Steuer, Abgabe

to punish
bestrafen

1 Use an acrostic to summarize some information from the text in your history folder. Start like this:

T *ax*
I
T
H
E

2 Read the text and think about symbols/arrows/shapes that you could use to illustrate the information from the text (below you find some examples on how these symbols could look like). Now draw a diagram which illustrates and summarizes the structure of society and the different obligations and duties.

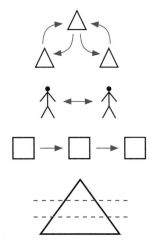

3 You are a lord. Make a poster with rules for the villeins.

4 Form three large groups. Each group works on a freeze frame which visualizes the social system of feudalism. Show your freeze frame to the other two groups.

Working in a medieval village

Meet the people in a medieval village.

to forge iron: Eisen schmieden | to herd: hüten | to carry: tragen | horseshoe: Hufeisen | tongs: Zange | tool: Werkzeug | earthen stove: Lehmofen | sack: Sack | corn: Getreide | water mill: Wassermühle | ox/oxen: Ochse/Ochsen | Feuer: fire | bread paddle: Brotschieber | anvil: Amboss | stick: Wanderstock

1 Look at the picture. Describe what jobs or professions you can see.

2 Find the different jobs around a medieval village in the word snake. Use a dictionary and look up words you don't know.

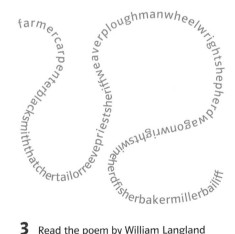

3 Read the poem by William Langland – written about 600 years ago – in silence. Then work with a partner: whisper the poem together, read it like an old woman/man, read it like somebody who is in power, who is in love, hungry, worked in the fields, …

Perform it in class and let your audience guess your way of reading.

The Crede of Piers the Ploughman
As I went on my way,
I saw a poor man over the plough bending.
His hood was full of holes,
And his hair was sticking out,
His shoes were patched.
His toes peeped out as he the ground trod.
His wife walked by him
In a skirt cut full and high.
Wrapped in a sheet to keep her from the weather.
Bare foot on the bare ice
So that the blood flowed.
At the field's end lay a little bowl,
And in there lay a little child wrapped in rags
And two more of two years old upon another side.
And all of them sang a song
That was sorrowful to hear.
The all cried a cry,
A sorrowful note.
And the poor man sighed sore and said
'Children be still.'

Piers the Ploughman, Trinity College Library, Cambridge. Chris Trueman (adapted): http://www.historylearningsite.co.uk/poor_peasant.htm

plough, plow: Pflug | hood: Kapuze, Kappe | toes: Zehen | patched: geflickt | he trod: er trat | wrapped: eingepackt | bare foot: barfüßig | rags: Lumpen | sorrowful: sorgenvoll, betrübt | sigh: seufzen

Winter, spring, summer and fall – Peasants at work

to sow: säen | to cut: schneiden | to herd: hüten | to shear: scheren | to thresh: dreschen | to tie sheaf/sheaves: Garben binden | to harvest: ernten | to slaughter: schlachten | to feed: füttern | to plant: pflanzen | to dig: graben

Calendar: 12 Scenes of the Labours of the Year, from 'Le Rustican' by Pietro de Crescenzi (1230–1320/21).

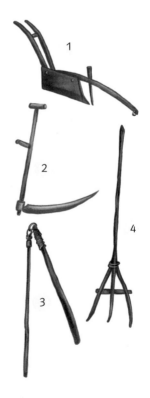

Life and work in a medieval village depended on the **seasons**. Peasants lived and worked in harmony with the seasons. Until the 12th century oxen were used to pull **ploughs**, then the use of horses spread, and their greater strength made farming more efficient. Working in the field was very exhausting and many tools were needed.

1 Explain what the first sentence of the text to the left means, using the illustration.

2 Imagine you are one of the people in the picture. Write a diary entry about your day and your feelings.

3 Copy the table into your history folder. Thereby bring the English terms, the German words, the descriptions and the numbers of the pictures into the right order.

Farming tools			
English term	**German word**	**Description of farming tool**	**Number of picture**
wood plough/plow	Heugabel/Forke	mow grass	…
scythe	Dreschflegel	cut and turn the earth	…
flail	Holzpflug	turn the drying grass to make hay	…
haymaking fork	Sense	separate grain from harvested sheaves	…

What did people eat?

Medieval recipe books are a good source of information on what medieval peasant families ate. They had a limited range of food: they often had stew or soup, mostly out of one pot, with bread and water. Most people had to make and preserve their own food. Except for manors and castles, houses did not have cool cellars, so food could not be kept for long. Fruit was cooked, meat was salted, dried or smoked.

1 There are nineteen words in the word jumble. Find ten of them. They tell you what people ate in medieval times.

recipe: Rezept | preserve: einwecken, einmachen | cellar: Keller | meat: Fleisch | salted: gesalzen | dried: getrocknet | smoked: geräuchert | ingredients: Zutaten

A	C	F	E	L	M	U	S	H	R	O	O	M	S	O	B
P	H	M	G	R	U	E	B	R	E	A	D	C	P	B	E
P	E	I	G	W	A	L	A	L	E	L	A	H	I	E	R
L	R	L	S	B	L	E	S	R	P	I	W	I	N	A	R
E	R	K	L	E	E	F	O	C	I	L	S	C	A	N	I
S	U	N	U	T	S	C	U	O	A	T	R	K	C	S	E
F	I	S	H	N	P	R	P	E	S	C	G	E	H	A	S
P	O	R	K	C	A	B	B	A	G	E	N	N	R	L	Z
R	A	D	I	S	H	E	S	S	C	A	R	R	O	T	S

2 Match the English words from the word jumble with the German words in the pot below.

Spinat Kirschen Fisch Milch
Hafer Eier Kohl
Radieschen Karotten
Pilze Roggenbrot
Hühnchen Bier Nüsse
Äpfel Schweine Bohnen
Suppe Beeren

3 Sort the words from the word jumble into the following categories:

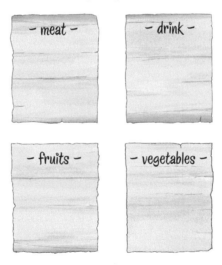

- meat -

- drink -

- fruits -

- vegetables -

4 What did you eat yesterday? Make a list.
What do you think that people in the Middle Ages could also have had? Tick the food in your list.

5 Interview your parents, grandparents, relatives or friends who can cook and create a menu for a medieval family dinner or lunch. What would you cook with the ingredients that you found above? Report in class.

Festivities and celebrations in a village in the Middle Ages

pole: Pfahl | playing dice: Würfel spielen | argument: Streit | weapon: Waffe | round dance: Reigen | stride: schreiten | hop: hüpfen | masquerade: Maskerade | floral wreath: Blumenkranz | fool: Narr | bagpipe: Sackpfeife/Dudelsack | flute: Flöte | knickerbockers: Kniebundhose | rooster: Hahn | vest/waistcoat: Veste/Wams | bench: Bank | feast: Feier

Medieval villagers performing a nose dance during a celebration. Woodcut, 1534, by Hans Sebald Beham (1500–1550).

KEY TERMS

gathering
Zusammenkunft/ Treffen

festivity
Feier/Fest

celebration
Feier

feast
Fest/Festessen

harvest
Ernte

to marry
heiraten

church
Kirche

Whitsun
Pingsten

mystery plays
Mysterienspiele

baptism
Taufe

wedding
Hochzeit

burial
Beerdigung

celebrate
feiern

1 Look at the picture. Close your eyes and tell your partner what you remember.

2 Imagine you are one of the people in the picture. What did you say or think at that moment? Share your ideas.

3 Read the texts and match the following words to the gaps.

until | flower | year | grandparents | everybody | presents | farming work

In a medieval village, _1_ knew everybody, and for all celebrations all the village people were invited. Most celebrations took place in summer because the houses did not have enough space, so the **gatherings** happened outside. **Festivities** and **celebrations** meant a change in the daily routines and they were repeated year after year. There were family, church, holy and seasonal days. Every _2_ the lord invited the peasants to a **feast** after handing over the payments, to celebrate a good **harvest**, when a baby was born in the lord's family or when someone in his family got **married**. Many festive days included a church service, sometimes processions, feasts and dancing, which served to increase the sense of community within the village.

Church days
Church feasts were occasions when peasants laid down their _3_ and went to mass. There were Easter, **Whitsun**, Thanksgiving and Christmas among other days. A twoweek Christmas vacation was the biggest feast. Houses were decorated with holly and ivy. The lord of the manor handed over _4_ to the villagers, like food, clothes, or wood. Sometimes **mystery plays** were preformed in church to tell stories from the Bible.

Baptisms

Baptizing a child meant washing away human sins and getting rid of everything evil. This celebration welcomed the new-born child in society. The _5_, friends and relatives were invited to church a few days after the child was born.

Weddings

Children of peasant families usually stayed with their families until they married. **Weddings** included simple ceremonies but great feasts with a lot of food. If villeins got married against the lord's will, they had to pay a fine. Most marriages were arranged _6_ the 18th century.

Burials

Burial sites were right in the middle of villages. The places in front of the church and the cemetary were also used for gatherings, games, and dances to flutes and drums.

Seasonal days

Seasonal days comprised days that were used to celebrate occasions around the farming year. For example on Plow Monday the freemen joined in a _7_ and competed to get as many lines as possible while children asked for pennies. If they did not get any they ploughed the front yard.

Maypole dancing

On May 1st a tree was cut down and used as a May Pole decorated with ribbons and _8_ garlands. People danced around it to **celebrate** the day. In some areas peasant boys gathered twigs from the woods and hung them in front of the window of a girl they liked.

3 Use a pencil and draw a picture into your history folder that sketches three of the festivities you just read about.

4 Describe the difference between your family festivities and those you have read about.

Growing up in a medieval village

KEY TERMS

chore
Pflicht, Haus- oder Routine-
arbeit

Peasant children from a medieval village did not go to school. As soon as they could walk they followed their parents in their daily routines and had to help with the **chores**.
Lacking specific playgrounds, they played whereever it was convenient: by or in the fields, in the house or yard or in the streets.

1 Copy the draft below into your history folder. Sort the activities for children according to their age in the yellow box. Write them into the speech bubbles or boxes.

2 Take a look at the different quoted activities. Form at least five complete sentences. Discuss with a partner.

3 What would you like to ask a medieval child? Write down your questions. Get together with a partner, talk about your questions, use them and write an interview of a medieval child. Read your interview in front of the class.

stayed at home alone when parents worked in the fields | watched young children | worked on the fields | helped with chores at home | helped prepare food | hunted birds | collected stones in the fields | collected eggs | helped with weeding | swept the house | collected fruit | milked cows | tended the garden | helped with brewing | got water from the river | watered the plough horses | looked after the animals | followed parents around | helped with ditch digging | helped with repairs | helped with road work

Check your knowledge

1 Copy the statements into your history
folder. Fill in the missing information, talk
about the solutions in class and find out
your score.

1. Village houses were made of _____.
2. People drank _____.
3. Festivities in a medieval village comprised _____.
4. Villagers did not only work on their own fields but they also had to _____.
5. Villages often had _____.
6. I know the following jobs in a medieval village: _____.
7. Farming tools that were used on fields in medieval times were: _____.

Your score

7 points: You are a history wiz.

5–6 points: Excellent, you were obviously concentrating!

3–4 points   Good, just a little bit more work needed.

1–2 points: More effort next time, please.

0 points: You have to take a look at the texts in this module again.

Create: Be a tour guide

You are a guide in a museum for the Middle
Ages. There, you walk your guests around.
With your knowledge from this chapter
create a tour and tell the visitors about how
people lived in a medieval village. Prepare
your tour and prepare notes. Bring pictures
you found in your German history book,
other books, or the internet.

1 Get together in groups of 4 or 5 and
walk your guests through your museum.

Teenagers at a museum for the Middle Ages.

2 Copy the feedback below chart into
your history folder. After the tour give
feedback to your guide. Fill in the feedback
in your guide's chart. Use ++, +, + -, -, --.

Feedback chart for _____ (Fill in your name.)			
	guest's name	guest's name	guest's name
interesting information			
pictures			
use of language			
What I also wanted to say:			

2 Medieval Cities and Citizens

Perhaps you have noticed it in the names of places, buildings and streets: many towns and cities in Germany, and in fact all over Europe, have a medieval history. Although they all look different, and even did so in medieval times, all of them had a great deal in common. Since many medieval cities are now destroyed or have changed greatly since, it is often difficult for us to understand how they were once organised.

On the following pages you are going to find out where towns and cities were founded in the first place, for what reason, and what medieval towns generally looked like. You will get to know the most important places in a medieval City, what kind of people lived there as well as what their work or occupation was.

1 Take notes: What activities at a medieval market can you see in the picture? Then let your partner choose a scene and explain it to him with the help of the vocabulary and the toolbox. Then you choose a scene and let your partner explain it.

2 Imagine you were a time-traveller to a medieval market. Write down in a report for your classmates what you can see, hear and smell.

3 Image you were listening to one of the conversations between two or more participants at this medieval market. In partner or group work, write down what they say. Then perform the conversation in class.

4 Go to your local farmer's market and compare: In what ways were medieval markets similar to and different from markets nowadays?

> **TOOLBOX: Describing actions**
>
> **to offer**
> anbieten
>
> **to transport**
> transportieren
>
> **to weigh**
> wiegen
>
> **to produce**
> herstellen
>
> **to entertain s.o.**
> jmd. unterhalten
>
> **to haggle**
> feilschen

At a medieval market.

pottery: Keramik | balance/scale: Waage | lute: Laute | hay: Heu | straw: Stroh | keg: Bottich | basket: Korb | handcart: Handkarren | headscarf: Kopftuch | stall: Marktstand

Where and why were medieval towns founded?

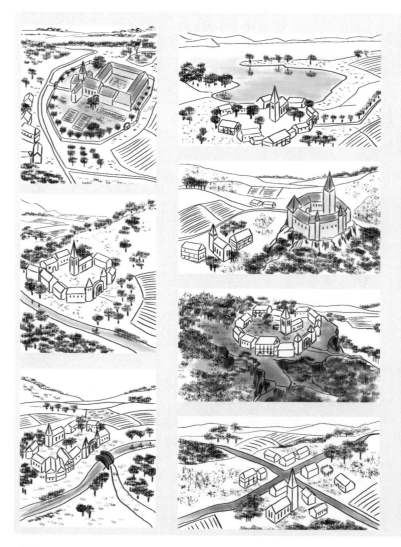

The majority of medieval cities and **towns were founded** between the 11th and 14th century by feudal lords on their own land. As feudal lords became richer, they started to buy many luxurious products from foreign **merchants**. **Fairs** or **markets**, where a greater number of people gathered, developed. **Artisans**, who made various items for their own as well as their lord's needs, were allowed to trade here with their products. With the permission of the **landlord**, these artisans also settled in such places, which often developed into economic and cultural centres.

1 Make a rough copy of the pictures below into your history folder and match them with at least one of the phrases on the right.

2 Discuss the results in class: Why did the landlords choose the different locations to found a city?

3 Very often the names of towns remind us of the reason why they were established. Find examples and collect them on the board.

monastries
nuns and monks needed supplies

water (rivers and streams)
good supply of fish; needed every day and people did not want to walk miles for it

fords/bridges
many travellers and traders, tax for using it

bays
protection of ships against storms, habour helped in trade

high ground
good view of the surrounding area; made it possible to spot enemies early and to prepare own defence

castles
defence against enemies

crossroads
many people/travellers/traders

How were medieval towns structured and organised?

1 Split up into different groups. Each group should take notes on the following questions. When you are finished, write a summary of your results in your file. Each group should then present the results of at least one question to the class.

a) Describe the **ground plan** of the town of Cologne during the Middle Ages in general. (Where was it founded? What form did it have? How was it protected?)

b) What could have been the reasons that it was founded just here by the Romans?

c) Which constructions from Roman times do you notice? In contrast, what are typical buildings and **characteristics** of a medieval town?

d) What developments in Cologne during the Middle Ages do you notice? What could have been the reasons?

e) What is a ghetto? Who might have had to live there?

2 Find a ground plan of another German medieval town (Nuremburg, Regensburg, Augsburg etc.) on the internet. Compare your results to this ground map. What seem to be **common** characteristics of medieval towns?

3 Compare the ground plan above to a plan of Cologne today. Which great **remnants** from the Middle Ages do you recognise? Report about them in class.

4 Find out about how your town or city looked during the Middle Ages. Which remnants from medieval times can you still discover today?

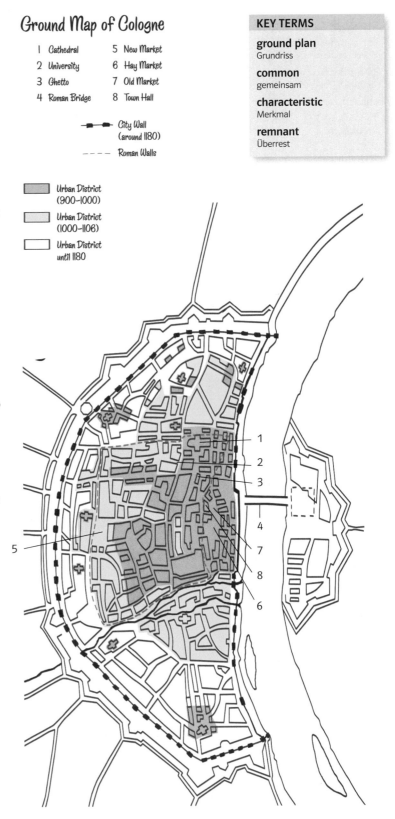

Ground Map of Cologne

1	Cathedral	5	New Market
2	University	6	Hay Market
3	Ghetto	7	Old Market
4	Roman Bridge	8	Town Hall

— City Wall (around 1180)

- - - - Roman Walls

Urban District (900–1000)

Urban District (1000–1106)

Urban District until 1180

KEY TERMS

ground plan
Grundriss

common
gemeinsam

characteristic
Merkmal

remnant
Überrest

Social order in medieval towns

1 Explain the chart below on the **social order** in medieval cities.

KEY TERMS

social order
Gesellschaftsordnung

councillor
Ratsherr

citizen
Bürger

inhabitant
Einwohner

dishonest
unehrlich

Jew
Jude

tradesman
Händler

craftsman
Handwerker

chandler
Krämer

civil servant
Beamter

profession
Beruf

inferior/superior
tiefer-/höhergestellt

servant
Bediensteter

beggar
Bettler

society
Gesellschaft

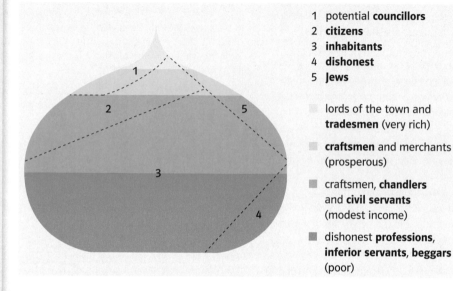

1 potential **councillors**
2 **citizens**
3 **inhabitants**
4 **dishonest**
5 **Jews**

lords of the town and **tradesmen** (very rich)

craftsmen and merchants (prosperous)

craftsmen, **chandlers** and **civil servants** (modest income)

dishonest **professions**, **inferior servants**, **beggars** (poor)

2 Which of the pictures fits to which social class in the diagram on medieval town-**society?** Give reasons for your choice.

3 Imagine one of the people from the pictures could talk. What do you think he or she would tell us?

Who governed the medieval towns?

1 Read the text on the right and write a brief description of how government worked in a medieval town.

2 Describe and explain the changes in medieval city **governance** from the 11th to the 14th century.

3 Find out about the duties and responsibilities of the mayor and city administration nowadays. Then compare them to those in the Middle Ages.

Townspeople in medieval times had the **privilege** of being able to run their own affairs via the **town council**, through a royal **charter** granted by the monarch. But over time, the way how the town was **governed** changed. The power shifted from the landlord to the people. But this did not always happen. Some towns were under the power of their landlord for hundreds of years.

The historian Peter Hammond about life in a medieval town
The medieval town had a defined hierarchy and those with the most power had the greatest say in how the town was run. The townspeople were answerable only to a town government. Charters were a good source of income for medieval monarchs, as a town paid to buy its charter, then made annual payments for the right to continue self-governing. Once the townspeople had been granted a charter, they were free **to elect** their own officers to run the town government. Those who elected the officers of the town council were the **freemen** – usually full members of one of the town's craft guilds. The council was headed by a **mayor**, again elected by the freemen.

Peter Hammond, Life in a Medieval Town, Amberley 2008,
© Stroud: Sutton 2007.

defined: festgelegt | hierarchy: Hierarchie | to be answerable to: verantwortlich sein gegenüber | craft guild: Gilde/Zunft (Vereinigung bzw. Körperschaft von Handwerkern) | to be headed by: angeführt sein von

KEY TERMS

governance
Regierung

city/town council
Stadtrat

charter
Gründungsurkunde, Freibrief

to govern
regieren

to elect s.o.
jemanden wählen

freeman
Freier, Ehrenbürger

mayor
Bürgermeister

administration
Verwaltung

jurisdiction
Rechtsprechung

welfare
Fürsorge

taxes
Steuern

laws
Gesetze

alliances
Bündnisse

treaties
Verträge

Foundation of medieval cities (11th century)	City self-governance (12th century)	City self-governance (14th century)	
ruler of the town (king, duke, earl or bishop)	mayor	mayor	city administration
↓ appoints	↑ elect	↑ elect	↑
burgrave, reeve or bailiff	aldermen (city council)	aldermen (city council)	
↓ governs	↑ elect noblemen or rich merchants (patricians)	↑ elect noblemen and members of guilds (freemen)	
townspeople	citizens (members of guilds)	citizens (members of guilds)	

Development of medieval town governance (11th–14th century) – duties and responsibilities of the medieval mayor and town council: ***administration****,* ***jurisdiction****,* ***welfare****,* ***taxes****,* ***laws****, war, peace,* ***alliances****,* ***treaties****, buildings, fire protection, control of epidemics*

duke: Herzog | earl: Graf | to appoint: ernennen | burgrave: Burggraf | reeve: Vogt | bailiff: Büttel (Verwalter) | alderman: Ratsherr | patrician: Patrizier | guild: Gilde/Zunft (Vereinigung bzw. Körperschaft von Handwerkern) | duty: Aufgabe, Obliegenheit | fire protection: Brandschutz | control of epidemics: Seuchenbekämpfung

The town council of Augsburg

1 Describe and analyse the picture in terms of what you have learned about medieval town governance. The vocabulary 'how to talk about pictures' in the inner cover might help you. Which groups of people and individuals do you notice? What significance do the three objects in the centre (town **seal**, town **keys** and bible) have?

2 Imagine the people in the painting could talk. Write down their conversation, and then perform it as a play in class.

KEY TERMS

seal
Siegel

key
Schlüssel

representative
Abgeordneter

participation
Teilnahme

significance: Bedeutung | illumination: (hier) Buchmalerei | to deliver: abliefern

Town Council of Augsburg (illumination, 16th century). **Representatives** of the guilds deliver demands for a **participation** in town governance (1368).

The guild: A craftsman's organisation

1 Read the following two sets of regulations of **craft guilds**. Then work with a partner: Write down an answer to the question 'What is a medieval craft guild?'

2 Outline the functions of a guild by explaining the aim of the different **regulations**.

The regulations of the craft guild of garment cutters of Stendal (1231):
1. No one shall presume to cut cloth, except if he is of our craft; those who break this rule will pay three talents to the guild.
2. Three times a year there must be a meeting of the brethren. Whoever does not come to it will pay what is right.
3. Whoever wishes to enter the fraternity, whose father was a brother and cut cloth will come with his friends to the meeting of the brethren. If he behaves honestly, he will be able to join the guild at the first request on payment of five solidi, and he will give six denarii to the **master**.
6. If any brother prepares cloth in his house and cuts or sells it at the wish of others, he will either cease or have no part in this fraternity.
8. Every year a master and four other good men who shall preside over the affairs of the guild will be faithfully chosen.

Adapted and simplified from: F. Keutgen, Urkunden zur Städtischen Verfassungsgeschichte, Berlin 1901, pp. 356–357.

garment cutter: Kleidungsschneider | to presume: sich erdreisten | talent: Taler | brethren: Brüder; hier: Mitglieder der Gilde | fraternity: Bruderschaft | request: Antrag | solidi: Solidus (mittelalterliches Zahlungsmittel) | denarii: Denar (mittelalterliches Zahlungsmittel) | to cease: aufhören | to preside over: den Vorsitz innehaben | affairs: Angelegenheiten | faithfully: ehrlich

Ordinance from the Southampton Guild Organisation (14th century):
6. And if a **guildsman** is ill and is in the city, wine shall be sent to him, two loaves of bread and a gallon of wine and a dish from the kitchen. And two approved men of the guild shall go to visit him and look after his condition.
7. And when a guildsman dies, all those who are of the guild and are in the city shall attend the service of the dead. And the guildsmen shall bear the body and bring it to the place of burial.

Adapted and simplified from: R. B. Morgan, Readings in English Social History from Contemporary Literature – Volume Four 1603–1688, Yutang Press 2007, p. 338. © Cambridge University Press, Cambridge 1922 (original publication)

a loaf of bread: ein Laib Brot | gallon: Gallone (Maßeinheit) | disk: Gericht | approved: anerkannt | condition: Zustand | to attend: (hier) beiwohnen | Service of the dead: Begräbnis | bear: tragen | place of burial: Grabesstätte

3 Each craft guild had its own coat of arms. Identify the coat of arms of the following guilds among the emblems:

KEY TERMS

craft
Handwerk

guild
Gilde/Zunft

regulation
Bestimmung, Regelung, Verfügung

master
Zunftmeister

ordinance
Satzung; Bestimmung; Erlass

guildsman
Zunftgenosse

emblem: Emblem | carpenter: Tischler | blacksmith: Schmied | goldsmith: Goldschmied | shoemaker: Schuster | barber: Barbier | butcher: Fleischer | tailor: Schneider | brick layer: Maurer | potter: Töpfer

Medieval jurisdiction

Medieval punishments. Coloured woodcut from Ulrich Tenglers 'Laienspiegel', Augsburg 1512.

to behead s.o.: jmd. köpfen | to break s.o. on the wheel: jmd. rädern | to burn s.o.: jmd. verbrennen | to chop s.o. hand off: jmd. die Hand abschlagen | to cut s.o. ear off: jmd. das Ohr abschneiden | to drown s.o.: jmd. ertränken | to flog s.o.: jmd. auspeitschen | to hang s.o.: jmd. hängen | to quarter s.o.: jmd. vierteilen | to rack s.o.: jmd. strecken

KEY TERMS

jurisdiction
Rechtssprechung

punishment
Strafe

offence
Straftat, Vergehen

to execute s.o.
jmd. hinrichten

execution
Hinrichtung

torture
Folter

to torture s.o.
jmd. foltern

means of interrogation
Verhörmethode(n)

death penalty
Todesstrafe

1 Match the medieval **punishments** mentioned in the vocabulary box above with those shown in the picture.

2 With the help of the internet, find out which of the above-mentioned punishments was used for which offence in the Middle Ages. Explain your results to the class.

3 Comment on the regulations in the following text.

Medieval law and order

Law and order was very harsh in medieval England. It was believed that people would only learn how to behave properly if they feared what would happen to them if they broke the law. Even the smallest **offences** had serious punishments. Thieves had their hands cut off. Women who committed murder were strangled and then burnt. People who illegally hunted in royal parks had their ears cut off and high treason was punishable by being hung, drawn and quartered. There were very few prisons as they cost money and local communities were not prepared to pay for their upkeep. It was cheaper to **execute** someone for bad crimes or mutilate them and then let them go.

Most towns had a gibbet just outside of it. People were hung on these and their bodies left to rot over the weeks as a warning to the others. However, such violent punishments clearly did not put people off.

Adapted and simplified from: Yelland: http://www.school-history.co.uk/year7links/life/lawandorder.pdf

harsh: hart | thief: Dieb | to commit murder: einen Mord begehen | to strangle: erwürgen | high treason: Hochverrat | to draw: (hier) strecken | to quarter: vierteilen | community: Gemeinde | upkeep: Instandhaltung | to mutilate: verstümmeln | gibbet: Galgen

4 Find out in which countries today
a) **torture** is still used as a **means of interrogation**
b) the **death penalty** is still applied.
Take notes and report about them in class. Then write down how you personally feel and what you think about this.

The Jews: A privileged minority?

1 Read the following source and copy the most important phrases into your history folder. Discuss the results in class and give reasons for your choice.

Grant of Lands and Privileges to the Jews
In 1084 the Bishop of Speyer made the following promise to the Jews:
When I made the village of Speyer into a town, I thought I would increase the honour I was bestowing on the place if I brought in the Jews. Therefore I placed them outside the town and some way off from the houses of the rest of the citizens. Lest they should be too easily disturbed by the insolence of the citizens, I surrounded them with a wall. Now the place of their habitation I transferred to them on condition that they pay annually three and a half pounds of the money of Speyer. I have granted also to them full power to change gold and silver, and to buy and sell what they please. Besides this I have given them land of the church for a cemetery. Then also just as the judge of the city hears cases between citizens, so the chief rabbi shall hear cases which arise between the Jews or against them. The Jews shall maintain watches, guards and fortifications about their district. They may lawfully employ nurses and servants from among our people. Slaughtered meat which they may not eat according to their law they may lawfully sell to Christians, and Christians may lawfully buy it. Finally I have granted that they may enjoy the same privileges as the Jews in any other city of Germany.

http://www.fordham.edu/halsall/source/1084landjews.html
Adapted and simplified from: Wilhelm Altmann; Ernst Bernheim. Ausgewählte Urkunden zur Erläuterung der Verfassungsgeschichte Deutschlands im Mittelalter. Berlin 1904. p. 156. Reprinted in: Roy C. Cave; Herbert H. Coulson. A Source Book of Medieval Economic History. Milwaukee 1936; reprinted: New York 1965, pp. 101–102. Scanned by Jerome S. Arkenberg, Cal. State Fullerton. The text has been modernized by Prof. Arkenberg.

bestowing: gewähren | lest: damit nicht | insolence: Anmaßung, Frechheit | habitation: Wohnort | annually: jährlich | to grant: gewähren | cemetery: Friedhof | judge: Richter | chief rabbi: Oberrabbiner (Funktionsträger in der jüdischen Religion) | to arise: aufkommen | to maintain: unterhalten | fortifications: Befestigungen | slaughtered meat: geschlachtetes Fleisch

2 Draw a table with two columns in your history folder. In the first column, list all the regulations made by the Bishop of Speyer regarding the Jews.

3 With a partner, discuss possible reasons for these regulations. Do you think that the bishop really wanted to 'increase the honour of Speyer' by 'bringing in the Jews'? Write the reasons in the second column of your table. Then compare your results with those of other classmates or discuss them together in class with your teacher. Consider the text and the picture below.

In the Middle Ages, Jews were often not **tolerated** by the Christian population. Jews had to wear a yellow Jewish hat, yellow stain or yellow circle as part of their clothes to mark them as Jews. In some cases Jews were even threatened, injured and murdered by the rest of the population.

Jewish hat: Judenhut | yellow stain: Judenfleck | yellow circle: gelber Kreis | to threaten: bedrohen | to injure: verletzen

KEY TERMS

privileged
privilegiert

minority
Minderheit

grant
Genehmigung

to tolerate
tolerieren

Jews burned at the stake. Illumination from 1513.

The bubonic plague (Black Death)

1 Using the internet, prepare a report on the causes, origins and characteristics of the bubonic plague, called 'the Black Death'.

2 Using the text extracts a–c, summarize in your own words how the bubonic plague was able to spread so quickly throughout the whole of England. Then explain what this meant for the country and its people.

3 Group work: Do some further research on other dangerous and highly **contagious deseases** during the Middle Ages such as smallpox, typhus, dysentery, malaria, leprosy and anthrax. In a group work-puzzle, inform your classmates about their causes, effects and potential remedies.

4 When the plague spread, the Jews were persecuted and exterminated. They were accused of causing the bubonic plague by poisoning the wells. Using your knowledge on Jews in the Middle Ages, explain why they could so easily be made the scapegoats for this epidemic.

cause: Ursache | origin: Herkunft | smallpox: Pocken | dysentery: Ruhr | leprosy: Lepra | anthrax: Milzbrand | potential: potenziell | remedies: Abhilfemaßnahmen | persecuted: verfolgt | exterminated: ausgelöscht | poisoning: vergiften | scapegoat: Sündenbock

a) Sanitary conditions in medieval towns such as Bristol (1348):
Filth running in open ditches in the streets, fly-blown meat and stinking fish, contaminated and adulterated ale, polluted well water, unspeakable privies, **epidemic disease**, – were experienced indiscriminately by all social classes.

Richard Holt; Gervase Rosser: The English Medieval Town. Longman 1990. http://www.bbc.co.uk/history/british/middle_ages/black_01.shtml

filth: Schmutz, Unrat | ditches: Straßengraben | fly-blown: fliegenbedeckt | contaminated and adulterated ale: verunreinigtes und gepanschtes Bier | polluted well water: verschmutztes Brunnenwasser | unspeakable privies: scheußliche Abtritte (mittelalterliche Plumpsklos) | indiscriminately: willkürlich, wahllos

b) The arrival of the plague:
In this year, 1348, in Melcombe [...] two ships, one of them from Bristol, came alongside. One of the sailors had brought with him from Gascony the seeds of the terrible pestilence, and through him the men of that town of Melcombe were the first in England to be infected.

Grey Friar's Chronicle, Lynn 1852. http://www.bbc.co.uk/history/british/middle_ages/black_01.shtml

alongside: (hier) an Land kommen | sailor: Seemann | seeds: Samen | pestilence: Pest, Seuche

c) The spreading of the plague:
Then the dreadful pestilence made its way along the coast by Southampton and reached Bristol, where almost the whole strength of the town perished, as it was surprised by sudden death; for few kept their beds more than two or three days, or even half a day.

Henry Knighton, Chronicon 19th century. http://www.bbc.co.uk/history/british/middle_ages/black_01.shtml

dreadful: schrecklich, furchtbar | perished: dahinscheiden, sterben

A plague victim reveals the telltale buboe on his leg. From a 14th century illumination.

Check and Create: A medieval comic

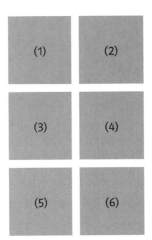

Online-Link
460082-0031
Figures of a medieval
comic strip.

a Create a comic strip about life in medieval towns: Think about a topic for your comic strip (e.g. a conversation between merchant and customer on the local market, a discussion between citizens about town governance, the arrival of the bubonic plague, the punishment of a local criminal etc.). The topic should enable you to use as much of the knowledge that you gathered in this module as possible.

b Print, copy or draw the characters in the right numbers and cut them out.

c Decide what should happen and be said in each scene on a separate sheet of paper.

d Divide a large piece of paper into the necessary number of squares for the different scenes of your comic.

e Place your figures into their correct positions. Then stick them onto the piece of paper. Finally, make them talk by adding speech bubbles and any necessary items.

(1)	(2)
(3)	(4)
(5)	(6)

3 Medieval Knights and Castles

Our ideas of a knight's life in the Middle Ages are often very romantic. We usually think of a knight as a brave and noble man in shiny plate armour. With a sword, colourful shield and banner he would fight in battles or try to win the heart of the lady he loved in a tournament. We usually imagine his castle to have been warm and cosy, with rich feasts taking place in the great hall in the evenings.

Although this might have been true for the lord of the castle, it certainly was not for the average knight. Who would think that his life was in reality very uncomfortable, hard and full of pain?

On the next pages, you will find out what life in a castle was actually like and what role knights played in medieval society.

1 Copy a rough sketch of the picture of the castle on the right into your history folder. Using the vocabulary beneath, number and label the different parts of the castle that you recognise.

2 With the help of the toolbox 'Describing life in a castle', take turns with a partner to say which parts of the castle you see, and explain their function. Note down in your sketch what your partner noticed in the cutaway.

3 Using your notes, explain to the class what you can generally say about life in medieval castles and their inhabitants.

4 Write down in keywords or key phrases what you know about knights and their life. Make a word field on a poster. Put it up in class, and at regular stages compare your results in this module with those on your poster.

TOOLBOX: Describing life in a castle

to plant
anbauen (z. B. Getreide)

to breed cattle
Viehzucht betreiben

to supply s.o. with sth.
jmd. mit etwas versorgen

to defend
verteidigen

to build up stocks
Vorräte anlegen

to guard
bewachen

to protect
(be)schützen

to store
aufbewahren

A medieval castle.

main building: Haupthaus | gate: Tor | drawbridge: Zugbrücke | stables: Ställe | cart: Wagen | barrel: Faß | banners: Fahnen | supplies: Vorräte | tower: Turm | well: Brunnen | curtain wall: Ringmauer | conical spire: Spitzturm | fixed bridge: feste Brücke | parapet walk: Wehrgang | moat: Burggraben | portcullis: Fallgatter | lower bailey: Vorhof | main bailey: Haupthof | chapel: Kapelle | round tower: Rundturm | crop: Ernte | field: Feld

Who stood where in the feudal system?

KEY TERMS

feudal system
Lehnswesen

villeins
abhängige Bauern/Leibeigene

higher noblemen
höhere Adelige

tenants-in-chief
Kronvasallen

peasants
Bauern

emperor
Kaiser

king
König

lower noblemen
niedere Adelige

bishop
Bischof

rank
Rang

knight
Ritter

clergyman
Geistlicher

shield
Schild

lance
Lanze

bow and arrow
Pfeil und Bogen

hierarchy
Rangordnung

hierarchic system
hierarchisches System

to be of higher/ lower rank than
von höherem/niederem Rang sein als

feudal lord: Lehnsherr | dukes: Herzöge | counts: Grafen | fief: Lehen | loyalty: Ergebenheit, Treue | obedience: Gehorsam | vasalls: Vasallen, Gefolgsmann | dues: Gebühren | tributes: Abgaben

The feudal pyramid.

1 Describe the scheme above and its people.

2 Fill the gaps 1–8 using the marked key terms.

This picture intends to show how medieval society functioned. The system is called the _1_. The highest feudal lord was a _2_ or _3_. He gave large parts of his land to _4_ (dukes, earls/counts, **bishops**). Because they received their fiefs (i.e. pieces of land) directly from the king, they were also called _5_. As a service in return they had to promise loyalty, obedience and military support to their feudal lord. These dukes, earls/counts and bishops again lent part of their land to other noble people of lower **rank** called _6_ (**knights** or barons). They were the vassals of the dukes, earls/counts and bishops and had to provide troops in cases of war. They also got dues/tributes from their vassals, the _7_, which they

then had to pass on to their feudal lords. Their vassals also had to take care of the properties of the nobility. Because some of them were not free, but belonged to the lord and were thus not allowed to leave the land, they were also called _8_ or villeins. They farmed the lord's land and had to give him much of the food. They were under the protection of the knights and stood at the lowest level of the feudal pyramid.

3 Work with a partner: Imagine you are a medieval peasant, and you have to describe the system you live in to a visitor. Your partner should then do the same in the role of a knight. Start like this:
'As a peasant, I am at the lowest level in medieval society. My lords are the lower noblemen (knights or barons). ...'

4 Discuss the positiv and the negative aspects of this system, and how it could have been changed to be fairer to the peasants.

Knighthood and chivalry

1 Using a dictionary, create a word field like the following for the knight that you see in the picture:

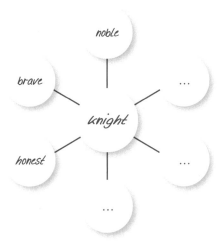

noble
brave
…
knight
honest
…
…

2 Read the following text of an English writer from the 12th century describing a knight. Explain what you get to know about medieval knights in your own words:

A youth must have seen his blood flow and felt his teeth crack under the blow of his adversary and have been thrown to the ground twenty times. Thus will he be able to face real war with the hopes of victory.

Cripps-Day, op. cit., p. 3. http://www.la84foundation.org/SportsLibrary/JSH/JSH1974/JSH0102/jsh0102b.pdf

> youth: Jüngling | blow: Hieb | adversary: Gegner | victory: Sieg

3 Find out about the **code of chivalry** by surfing the internet.

4 Think about how **to behave chivalrously** or **decently** today. Then create your own modern 'code of chivalry'. Write or print it onto a large poster, and hang it up in your classroom.

A shortened and simplified list of a knight's duties from the 'Charlemagne's Code of Chivalry' at the end of the 8th century:
To fear God
To serve his lord
To protect the weak and defenceless
To live by honour and for glory
To fight for the welfare of all
To guard the honour of other knights
To keep faith
At all times to speak the truth
To respect the honour of women

http://www.baronage.co.uk/chivalry/chival1a.html

KEY TERMS

knighthood
Rittertum

chivalry
Ritterlichkeit/Rittertum

code of chivalry
ritterlicher Ehrenkodex

to behave chivalrously
sich ritterlich benehmen

decent
höflich, anständig

How did a boy become a knight?

1 Read the paragraphs A to G. Look for key words in the sentences. Then put them into a logical order, and find out what the act of becoming a knight was also called.

2 Imagine you were a medieval knight who is telling his newly assigned page about the stages in his career. Start like this: 'When I was your age, I, as a nobleman's son, began my training as a knight at a neighbouring nobleman's castle. As a page, I spent most of my days strengthening my body, wrestling and riding horses …'

(A) N
The night before the ceremony, the **squire** dressed in a white **tunic** and red **robes**. He then fasted and prayed all night. The chaplain blessed the future knight's sword and then laid it on the altar of the **chapel** or church. Before dawn, the knight took a bath to show that he was pure, and he dressed in his best clothes. When dawn came, the priest heard the young man's **confession**. Then the squire ate breakfast.

(B) U
As a **page**, a boy spent most of his time strengthening his body, wrestling and riding horses. He learned how to fight with a spear and a sword. He was also taught to read and write by a schoolmaster. The lady of the castle taught the page his **manners**, how to sing and dance, and how to behave in the nobleman's **court**.

(C) I
Once a squire had proven himself worthy in battle, and his knight felt he was ready, he could become a knight himself. Squires were **knighted** in a **knighting ceremony** at about twenty years of age.

to fast: fasten | dawn: Morgendämmerung | to wrestle: ringen | to prove yourself worthy: sich als würdig erweisen | chaptain: Geistlicher

(D) B
A page could become a squire at the age of fifteen or sixteen. Each squire was then assigned to a knight. A knight could have several squires.

(E) B
A squire assisted the knight to whom he was assigned. His duties included dressing the knight in the morning, serving all of the knight's meals, caring for the knight's horse, and cleaning the knight's armour and weapons. He followed the knight to tournaments and assisted his lord on the battlefield. He prepared himself by learning how to handle a sword and lance while wearing forty pounds of armour and riding a horse.

(F) G
Then the ceremony began. It took place in front of the family, friends and the nobility. The squire knelt in front of the lord, who tapped the squire lightly on each shoulder with his sword and proclaimed him a knight. This was symbolic of what had happened in earlier times. In the earlier Middle Ages, the person doing the knighting actually hit the squire forcefully, knocking him over. After the ceremony, a great feast followed with music and dancing.

(G) D
At the age of seven or eight, a nobleman's son began training for knighthood at a neighbouring nobleman's castle as a page.

to be assigned to s.o.:
jmd. zugeteilt werden | to knee: knien | to proclaim s.o. as sth.: jmd. zu etw. ernennen | neighbouring: benachbart

How did a knight protect himself?

As you have learned on the last page, a squire would always help his master knight to dress in his **armour**. Armour and **weapons** changed in style throughout the long medieval period. Until the 14th century knights wore **chain mail** made out of about 200,000 small rings riveted or welded together, to protect themselves. Since these were rather heavy on the body and uncomfortable to wear, from the 14th century onwards knights wore **plate armour** that still weighed 45 to 55 pounds (approximately 20–25 kg).

1 Squire William wants to write an instruction manual for other squires on how to dress a knight properly. Unfortunately he is a beginner, so you need to help him write the manual. The way to dress a knight in the 15th century was to start dressing him from his feet upwards. Sort the following words first by looking at the picture on the left. Then write your manual. While doing so, also explain what the pieces of equipment were good for.

Start like this:
Dress your lord from his feet upwards. Start with his greaves. They protect his ...

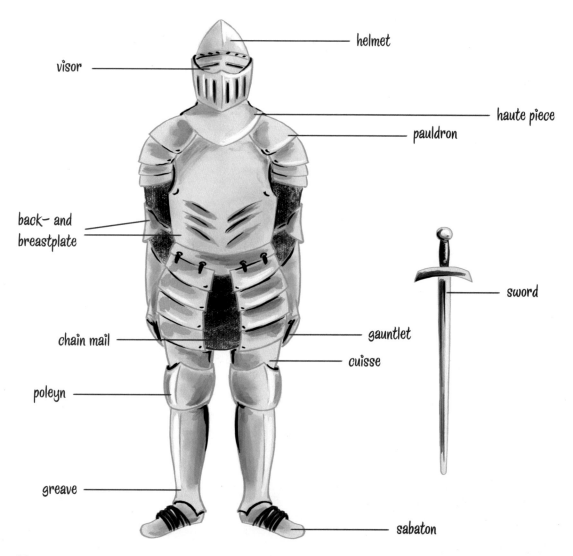

visor — helmet

haute piece

pauldron

back- and breastplate

sword

chain mail — gauntlet

cuisse

poleyn

greave — sabaton

Tournaments: The knight's great festivals

The medieval **tournament** developed around the 10th century. Knights wanted to practise their **horsemanship** and **weapons skills** outside of actual **battle**. As time went on, the tournament changed from a military exercise to a sporting competition and entertainment.

Tournaments became all-day events. They now included other activities such as **feasting** and dancing. Tournaments could be attended by anyone, including women and children. Wooden stands were built, decorated with colourful **pennants**, to seat the nobles.

The two favourite activities at the tournaments were the **melee** and the **joust**. The melee was a team sport. Each team of knights had coloured flags on their backs, which the opposite side tried to knock off using **clubs** and blunt swords.

The joust was a **combat** between two knights. A low wooden fence separated the knights. The two knights started on their horses, holding long lances. They rode towards each other, with their lances up and ready, each on their own side of the fence. The aim was to knock the **opponent** off his horse. Both the melee and the joust were hard sports in which many knights were injured or killed.

1 Analyse the picture using the information from the text and the 'Rules of the Joust'. Write your results down in your file.

KEY TERMS
tournament   Turnier
horsemanship   Reitkunst
weapon skills   Waffenfertigkeit
battle   Kampf
feasting   feiern
pennant   Banner/Wimpel
melee   Tumult/Handgemenge
joust   Tjost/Zweikampf
clubs   Knüppel
combat   Kampf
opponent   Gegner

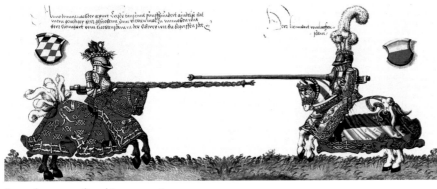

Scene from a mediaval tournament.

Rules of the Joust
1. *Only nobles may ride in a joust.*
2. *You must have your own horse and equipment.*
3. *You may use three lances in each jousting match. When your three lances have broken, the jousting match is over. (But knights usually continued their battle on foot using swords.)*
4. *You receive one point for breaking your lance on your opponent's chest.*
5. *You receive two points for breaking your lance on your opponent's helmet.*
6. *You receive three points for knocking your opponent off his horse. This ends the match.*
7. *When you fall, only your own squire may help you. When you break a lance, only your own squire may hand you a new one. Only your squire may talk to you during the match, and only when resetting your horse for the next attack.*

to attend s.th.: an etwas teilnehmen | blunt: stumpf | fence: Zaun | to separate: teilen | contemporary: zeitgenössisch

2 Work with a partner: Explain the joust and its rules in your own words.

3 Discuss: Which parallels – but also which differences – do you see between medieval tournaments and contemporary sports?

Attacking and defending a castle

Siege of a medieval castle.

1 Make a chart like the one below. Then match the words below describing the items on the picture with the right number or letter in the chart. Some words decribe items for attack as much as for defence.

drawbridge: Zugbrücke | burning projectiles: brennende Projektile | Greek fire: Griechisches Feuer (eine flüssige Brandwaffe) | guards: Wachen | ladder: Leiter | mantlet: Pluteus (hölzerner, mobiler Schutzschild) | moat (wet or dry): Burggraben | arrow slits: Schießscharten | battering ram: Rammbock | bridge: Brücke | catapult: Katapult | crossbow: Armbrust | round towers: Rundtürme | siege tower: Belagerungsturm | thick walls: dicke Mauern | trebuchet: Blide (großes Katapult mit Gegengewicht)

Attack	Defence
1 ...	A ...
2 ...	B ...
3 ...	C ...

2 Describe what the different items on the picture (p. 40) were used for.
For example: The catapult was a long-range offensive weapon. It was used to shoot large projectiles (for example stones) at a castle to destroy its buildings and walls.

3 Imagine you were a knight in the Middle Ages and that you either attacked or defended a castle today. Write a report on what you have seen, heard, smelled, and felt before, during, or after the attack. You could start like this:
Today we attacked Aberystwyth Castle. I felt very excited before the attack, because I was supposed to man the siege tower. When we arrived at the battlefield I saw …

4 Form three groups in class. The different groups should focus on doing some research in the internet on the following aspects.
Prepare to tell your classmates further details about your findings. Also remember to print illustrations for your report!

Group one: Different types of castles in the Middle Ages, their advantages and disadvantages (use the pictures to the right and the internet as well).

Group two: Different weapons and ways of attacking a castle, their advantages and disadvantages.

Group three: Different weapons and ways of defending a castle, their advantages and disadvantages.

offensive weapon: Angriffswaffe | defensive weapon: Verteidigungswaffe | protective means: Schutzmittel | long-range weapon: Fernkampfwaffe | short-range weapon: Nahkampfwaffe

The coat of arms: A knight's business card

Knights in plate armour could not be recognised on first sight. That is why they used **heraldry** to identify each other in jousts and on the battlefields. Heraldry includes the family's coat of arms and motto. Medieval knights used the **coat of arms** on their tabards, shields and banners to express their identity and status in society.

As time went on, a family's coat of arms was recorded so that no one could copy the pattern or take it for themselves. So today you can look up the name of a family and find their coat of arms in the old records. The study of these coats of arms is also called heraldry.

The design of a coat of arms followed a certain pattern, although each was different. First the knight had to choose the shape of the shield. The first step in the creation of the so called 'blazon' was to choose the 'ordinaire' (the geometrical shapes on the coat of arms). The second step then was to choose the colours of the 'ordinaire', each colour having a different meaning. The third step was then to choose the 'charges', basically speaking the items on the shield. These items again had a certain meaning.

Banner of King Edward III
Ordinaire: per cross (protection)
Colours: blue (loyality and truth);
            red (military strength and
            magnanimity)
Charges: lions (fearless courage);
            fleur-de-lis (i.e. lily flower;
            royal symbol)

1 Read the text on the left and write a brief explanation of the use of heraldry. Have a look at the coat of arms of Edward III. What can you say about him?

Medieval phrases and sayings

Although their original meanings may have changed over the years, many phrases and words still used in English were coined in the Middle Ages. Some of them refer to the living environment of the knights and knighthood. Some are similar and some very different to German sayings.

1 Try to match the following phrases to their original meaning in medieval times. Then try to explain what they mean today and find a similar German expression.

1) to give somebody the cold shoulder
2) Get off your high horse!
3) to throw down the gauntlet

A) A gauntlet was the glove in a suit of armour. Throwing down your gauntlet was a way of challenging somebody to a duel.

B) When unwanted visitors came you gave them this cold piece of mutton instead of hot meat as a hint that they were not to call again.

C) In the 13th century nobles were given a taller breed of horse to ride to express their status and authority. They would say this if one of them was acting more authoritatively than he had a right to.

'Go Online': The creation of an internet-website

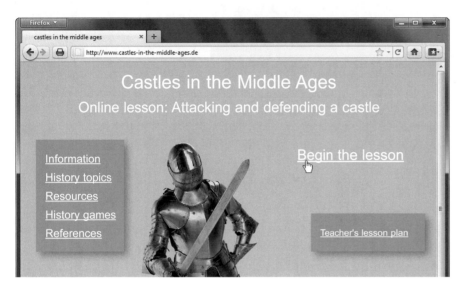

Creating your own internet-website on 'Medieval Knights and Castles' is easier than you might think. But remember: Planning is the first stage on your way to success! Therefore carry out the following steps before you start:

1 Divide your class into different groups. Each group should work on one webpage. Decide which subtopics you want to have (e.g. 'Castles in the Middle Ages', 'Life in a medieval castle', 'Attacking and defending a castle' etc.) and which group should work on which subtopic.

2 Now make an outline of your website in the form of a structure diagram. The structure of your website could look like this:

3 Do some research on your topic in the internet. First take notes. Then write your texts (in your own words!) in your history folder and have your teacher correct them. Do not forget to include illustrations.

4 Download a freeware html-editor that works on the principle 'What you see is what you get'.

5 Create your webpage and save it. After you have finished, give the HTML-file of your webpage to your teacher so he can open all the files in one document and link the pages. Publish your website on the internet by pressing the 'publish'-button. For that, you need an internet domain.

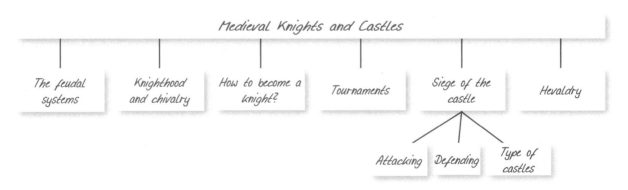

4 The Crusades – Holy Wars?

Jerusalem is the holy city for both Christians and Muslims. From the seventh century, Jerusalem and the surrounding area were ruled by the Muslims. In 1095 the Christians reported difficulties travelling to the Holy Land. The head of the Christian Church, Pope Urban II, called for volunteers to travel to Jerusalem and fight to take it back from the Muslims. Over the next 200 years Christians set out on crusades to control the Holy Land. In the end the Muslims managed to fight off the invading Christian armies and keep control of their land. In this module you can find out why the Christians went on crusades, how they captured Jerusalem and what resulted from the crusades.

1 The illustration on the right shows the crusaders conquering Jerusalem. Describe the picture to your partner. The toolbox and the vocabulary 'how to talk about pictures' in the inner cover might help you.

2 Work in groups and write down what else you would like to know about the picture and the crusades. Make one question poster for the class. The following pages will help you to find answers to some of those questions. For others, you might have to surf the Internet or ask your teacher.

TOOLBOX: Conquering a city
to conquer   erobern
to climb   klettern
city wall   Stadtmauer
armed   bewaffnet
shield   Schild
armour   Rüstung
sword   Schwert
siege tower   Belagerungsturm
to throw stones   Steine werfen

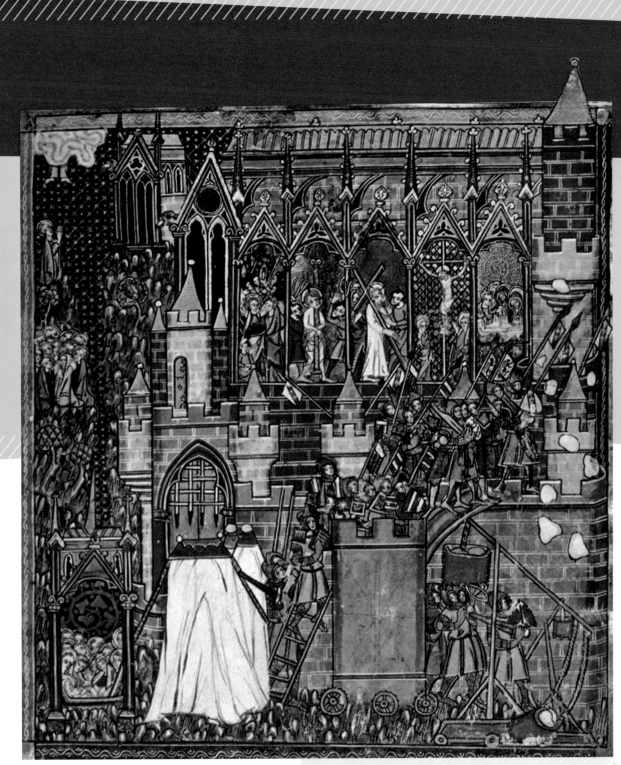

The siege of Jerusalem as depicted in a medieval manuscript from the 14th century.

Passion of Christ: Leidensgeschichte Christi | to arrest s.b.: jmdn. gefangen-nehmen | to flog s.b.: jmdn. auspeitschen | to be nailed to the cross: ans Kreuz genagelt werden | to be executed by crucifixion: am Kreuz hingerichtet | to bury s.b.: jmdn. beerdigen | to pray: beten | to ascend to heaven: in den Himmel hinaufsteigen

Why did people make long journeys in the Middle Ages?

KEY TERMS

pilgrimage
Pilgerreise

holy
heilig

shrine
Heiligtum

to pray
beten

to forgive
vergeben

sin
Sünde

to please
gefallen

adventurous
abenteuerlustig

pilgrims
Pilger

Palestine
Palästina

Muslim (adj.)
muslimisch

Muslim (noun)
Muslim

1 Read the text slowly. Write a question at the end of each sentence.

In the Middle Ages the Church encouraged people to make **pilgrimages** to special **holy** places called **shrines**. It was believed that if they **prayed** at these shrines, they might be **forgiven** for their **sins** and have more chances of going to heaven.
So to **please** God people went on pilgrimage, some of them even abroad.
The most **adventurous pilgrims** went to **Palestine**, to see the Holy Land where Jesus had lived.

As travelling on long journeys was dangerous in the Middle Ages, pilgrims often went in groups. Pilgrims going to Palestine had to travel through **Muslim** lands. They were often attacked by **Muslims**.

2 Pair work: Share your questions with your partner and answer your partner's questions.

3 Look at the picture. Describe what the people are doing.

4 Speculate on what the people are thinking. Write speech bubbles for them.

Pilgrims being attacked by Muslims.

The beginning of the crusades

KEY TERMS

to capture
einnehmen

Christian
Christ

to drive out
hinausjagen

duty
Pflicht

wealth
Wohlstand

fortune
Vermögen

invader
Eindringling

When the Muslim armies **captured** the holy city of Jerusalem in 1095 they stopped **Christian** pilgrims from visiting the holy places in the East. Pope Urban II wanted the Muslims **driven out** of the Holy Land. Most crusaders went because the Church said it was their **duty** as Christians. Others had heard of the great **wealth** of the East and hoped to make their **fortunes** there. Some went for excitement and adventure. For Muslims, the crusades were battles fought to defend their lands from foreign **invaders**. Whatever the reason for going, thousands of Christians answered Pope Urban's call to **fight** the holy war against the Muslims.

1 Read the text and start drawing a star diagram about the crusades. Fill in the star diagram with pieces of information from the text answering the w-questions.

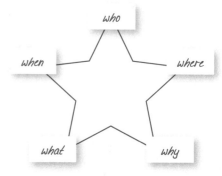

Pope Urban II at the Council of Clermont

Pope Urban II addresses a great crowd of **churchmen** and laymen at the Council of Clermont in 1295

Brothers, I speak as a messenger from God. Your fellow Christians in the east desperately need help. The Saracens have attacked them and have **pushed** deep into Christian land. They are killing great numbers of Christians. They are destroying churches and land. In the name of God, I **beg** you all to drive out these foul creatures.

Your own land has too many people. There is not much wealth here. The soil hardly grows enough to support you. Set out for Jerusalem. Take that land from the wicked **infidel** and make it your own. If you die on the journey or if you are killed in a **battle** against the Saracens all your sins will be forgiven at once. God Himself has given me the power to tell you this.

Byron, Jamie; Counsell, Christine; Riley, Michael; Medieval Minds, Britain 1066-1500, London 2001, p. 115. © Longman, London 1997 (Originalausgabe)

> layman: Laie | messenger: Bote | fellow Christians: Mitbrüder | Saracens: Sarazenen (historische Bezeichnung für Muslime) | foul: verdorben | soil: Ackerboden | wicked: boshaft

Pope Urban II at the Council of Clermont as depicted in a medieval book, 1490.

1 Find words/phrases in the source linked with Muslims and write them down. Compare your results with your neighbour and comment on your findings.

2 Analyse the speech. Make a grid as shown below and fill in the key words that answer the following questions.

3 Using the information you get from the painting of the Council of Clermont and Pope Urban's speech, write down the reasons why many people would go on a crusade after listening to Pope Urban's words.

4 Finish the star diagram you have already started on page 46 with the additional information from Pope Urban's speech.

Who delivered the speech?	...
Where was it delivered?	...
When was it delivered?	...
To whom was the speech addressed?	...
Why was it delivered?	...
What is the speech about?	...

An overview of the crusades

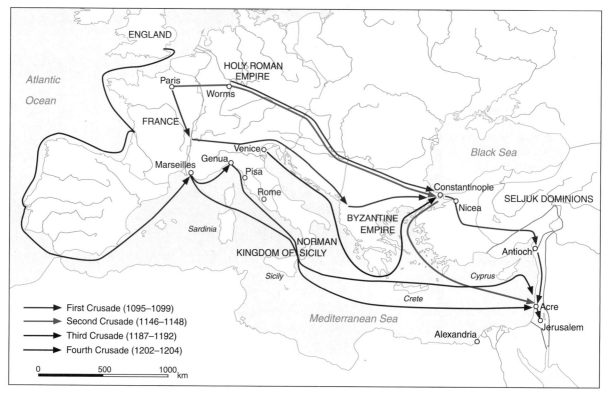

Paths of the crusaders.

There were eight major crusades which departed from Europe for the Holy Land between 1096 and 1291. During and immediately after the first crusade a number of knights set up small Christian states for themselves in the East. They were called the Crusader States. The first four states set up by the Christians were the County of Edessa, the Principality of Antioch, the Kingdom of Jerusalem and the County of Tripoli.

county: Grafschaft | principality: Fürstentum

1 Trace the path of the first crusades. Using an atlas, find out which modern countries each path passed through. Describe the paths to your partner using the vocabulary in the toolbox. The vocabulary 'how to talk about maps' in the inner cover might help you as well.

TOOLBOX: Talking about routes

to set off (on a crusade)
aufbrechen zu einem Kreuzzug

to pass s.th.
an etwas vorbeikommen

to make a stop in/at
Halt machen in/an

to set sail
in See stechen

to go ashore
an Land gehen

to arrive at
ankommen in

2 Calculate how many kilometers a pilgrim would travel from Cologne to Jerusalem.

The siege and capture of Jerusalem

When the crusaders finally reached Jerusalem in June 1099, they began attacking straight away, but made little progress. Also, there was a **rivalry** between two crusader leaders, Godfrey of Bouillon and Raymond of Toulouse. As Jerusalem had very solid walls, the crusaders started to build siege towers; the siege of Jerusalem had begun.

1 Copy the plan of Jerusalem and make notes about what happened at different places. Use the information from the following sources.

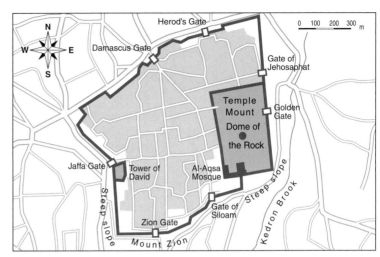

A plan of Jerusalem. The place upon which the Temple of Solomae formerly stood is known as the Temple Mount.

Gesta Francorum – the accounts of eye-witnesses and participants

Duke Godfrey **besieged** the city from the north side. Count Raymond and his army, however, settled down on the West and besieged Jerusalem from the camp of the Duke to the foot of Mount Zion. But since his men could not come close to besiege the wall, the Count wished to move his camp and change his position. Count Raymond brought his army and his tower up near the wall from the south.

August C.. Krey: The first Crusade: The accounts of Eyewitnesses and Participants, Princeton 1921, pp. 256–257.

> duke: Herzog | count: Graf

Gesta Francorum – the accounts of eye-witnesses and participants

But this time the pilgrims entered the city, pursuing and killing the Saracens up to the Temple of Solomon, where the enemy gathered in force. The battle raged throughout the day, so that the Temple was covered with their blood. When the pagans had been overcome, our men seized great numbers, both men and women, either killing them or keeping them captive [...] Afterwards, the army started looting the city.

August C.. Krey: The first Crusade: The accounts of Eyewitnesses and Participants, Princeton 1921, pp. 256–257.

> to pursue: verfolgen | to gather in force: sich in großer Stärke versammeln | to rage: toben | pagan: Heide | to seize: festnehmen | captive: gefangen | to loot: plündern

A Muslim scholar about the capture of Jerusalem

The Franks stayed in Jerusalem for a week, during which they killed the inhabitants. ... More than 70,000 Muslims were killed by the Franks in the Al-Aqsa Mosque, amongst them religious scholars and devout Muslims, who wanted to live piously in this holy place. The Franks also stole more than forty silver candlesticks from the Dome of the Rock ...

Francesco Gabrieli (ed.), Die Kreuzzüge aus arabischer Sicht, © 1973 Bibliographisches Institut/Artemis & Winkler, Mannheim; translated by H. Kremer.

> Franks: Franken | scholar: Gelehrter | devout: fromm | piously: fromm

KEY TERMS

rivalry
Wettstreit

siege
Belagerung

to besiege
belagern

2 Divide into groups. Choose one of the following perspectives from which to describe the capture of Jerusalem.
a) You are one of the crusaders. Write a letter to your family back in Europe describing the storming of Jerusalem. Use the eyewitnesses' accounts.
b) You are a Muslim who escaped from Jerusalem. After a long journey you finally arrive in Baghdad and tell your friends what you witnessed in Jerusalem.

3 Have a look at the painting of the siege of Jerusalem (p. 45) again. Explain whether you think the picture was taken from was a Muslim or a Christian manuscript.

What resulted from the crusades

By 1291 the Muslims were once again in control of the Holy Land and the last crusaders returned to Europe. As there were only a handful of major battles and sieges over the 200 years, many Christians learned to respect the Muslims. Some of them lived together, traded and shared ideas.

They learned how to build stronger castles and to study the stars. The returning crusaders brought goods from the East such as cotton, silk, sugar, perfume, carpets and spices like chilli, cinnamon, cloves, ginger, nutmeg and pepper.

They also benefited from the Eastern discoveries in science and mathematics. Arab numbers were easier to use than Roman numbers, and the Muslims knew much more about medicine.

1 Read the text. Find out what the Europeans gained from the Muslims and fill in the grid.

major: größere | to trade: handeln | silk: Seide | spices: Gewürze | cloves: Nelken | nutmeg: Muskat | to benefit from: profitieren von | discovery: Entdeckung

Treasures from the East					
Cloth	**Fortifications**	**Luxuries**	**New Ideas**	**Spices**	**Others**
…	…	…	…	…	…
…	…	…	…	…	…
…	…	…	…	…	…
…	…	…	…	…	…

cloth: Stoff | fortification: Befestigungsanlage | luxuries: Luxusgüter

Arab scholars at the deathbed of the Christian king William of Sicily (1166–1189), picture story 1196.

2 What were the 'treasures from the East' used for? Connect the new goods with the words on the right.

1. chilli   a. makes you smell nice
2. sugar   b. is used to make clothes
3. carpet   c. gives a hot taste to food
4. silk   d. gives flavour to sweet food
5. perfume   e. makes tea, coffee etc. sweeter
6. cinnamon f. covers floors or stairs

3 The picture showing Arab scholars at the deathbed of the Christian king William of Sicily shows a picture story. Write it down and don't forget to explain why the Christian king trusts the Arab doctor.

4 At home: Fill a basket with the new products from the East. In the classroom: Now be a merchant and try to sell your products to your classmates.

Check: Crossword puzzle

1 Look at the following word bubbles. What evidence could each speaker use to support his views?

Create: Radio documentary

Group work - creating a radio documentary about the crusades

A radio station has asked you to create a radio documentary about the crusades. Therefore you need to revise your material, write a script and decide which sound effects you may want to use.

Your radio documentary should include the following elements:
• reports about the important events,
• interviews,
• music or sound effects.

Your ideas should always take your audience into account (e.g. Christian or Muslim listeners).

Once you've thought of your basic idea, get back to the material and mark all the important information. Write a script for your radio documentary together and don't forget to let your teacher proof-read your work. Rehearse your documentary and finally record it!

Your radio documentary will be as assessed on the following criteria:
✓ historical information – are facts correct and the important ones included ?
✓ authenticity – do people stay in character?
✓ recording – are voices, sounds and music audible?

5 Monasteries and Convents in the Middle Ages

In medieval times, the Christian religion and the belief of heaven and hell was much more important than nowadays. Living a strictly-organized and simple way of life in a monastery or a convent as a monk or a nun was believed to be the best way to go to heaven after death. In the 14th century there were about 5,000 monks and 3,500 nuns in England. Numerous monasteries and convents were built. Their ruins and those still standing bear witness to their importance at that time.

So, what was day-to-day life like for monks and nuns? What did a monastery look like? What rooms did a convent have? In this chapter you find out about the various occupations of monks and nuns and the importance of monasteries and convents in society.

1 Get together with a partner. Describe one of the scenes in the French illumination. Your partner makes a rough sketch of what you describe. Before you start, take some time to look at the picture and think of words you need. Use the vocabulary under the picture and the vocabulary 'how to talk about pictures' in the inner cover. Swop roles and use another scene.

2 Write down all the words that you can think of when looking at the picture.

3 What would you like to ask the people in the picture, what would you like to know about the time? Formulate question.

4 Use the activity box as help to act the picture.

ACTIVITY BOX: Act the picture

1 Get together with a group up to six.

2 Decide which part of the picture you will act out.

3 Decide together who will be your director. He/She positions you following the picture.

4 Stay frozen for 30 seconds.

5 The director gives a sign and you start moving and talking as the persons in the picture.

6 Practice a few times.

7 Present your work.

French manuscript illumination, c. 1300, showing nuns celebrating mass in a convent (above), and a procession through the convent's cloister (below).

Why did people become monks and nuns?

There were different reasons for people to enter a monastery or convent. In order to become monks or nuns, children could enter a monastery or convent at the age of 7. They were then **novices – apprentice** monks and nuns. Later they had to take the vows if they wanted to stay in the monastery or convent.

Sometimes, **orphans** were handed over to monasteries when families could not look after them. Some families had too many children and thus gave one or more to the nuns so they would not **starve**. Sometimes also girls who were not married but got **pregnant** were hidden in convents. For women, convents offered a way to go to school. They provided the only source of education for women.

Orderic Vitalis (about 1075–1140) wrote about how he became a monk:
And so, o glorious God, you dist inspire my father Odeleric to renounce me utterly and submit me … thy governance. So, weeping, he gave me, a weeping child, into the care of the monk Reginald, and sent me away into exile for the love of thee, and never saw me again. And I, a mere boy, did not … oppose my father's wishes, but obeyed him …, for he promised me … if I became a monk I should taste the joys of Heaven … after my death. … And so, a boy of ten, I crossed the English channel and came into Normandy …, unknown to all, knowing no one … I heard a language I could not understand. … I was received as an oblate in the abbey of St Evroul by the … abbot Mainier in the eleventh year of my life … The name Vitalis was given me in place of my English name, which sounded harsh to the Normans.

Adapted from: M. Chibnall, ed. and trans. (1972), The Ecclesiastical History of Orderic Vitalis, Oxford: OUP. Found in: Mc Kay, J. P., Hill, B. D. & Buckler, J. (1991), A History of Western Society, Vol. 1. From Antiquity to the Enlightenment, Boston et al., p. 299.

1 Summarize in your own words how Orderic became a monk. Summarize his feelings.

The vows – the first step to become a monk or a nun

If you wanted to stay at a convent you had to follow certain rules and take the vows of the respective religious order, such as the Benedictines, the Dominicans, the Cistersians, the Carmelites, and more. Many monasteries and nunneries in the Middle Ages followed the rules set down by St Benedict in the sixth century. The monks and nuns became known as Benedictines and took three main vows:
The **vow** of **poverty**,
the vow of **chastity**, and
the vow of **obedience** to their leaders.
That meant that monks and nuns did not own anything, did not get married or have a partner, and followed the rules of the convent and the church community.

1 Do you have plans and aims and ambitions for your life? Write down your own vow, promises for yourself. Make a nice frame around it. Perhaps you can use a quill and ink. If you like, you can share them with your classmates.

A nun taking her vows and mass preformed by a bishop.

The prayers – speaking to God

The daily life of medieval monasteries and convents centered around the hours. The Book of Hours was the main prayer book and was divided into eight sections, or hours. These were read at specific times of day. Every part contained **prayers**, **psalms**, and **hymns**. Monks and nuns went to church eight times a day to sing and **recite** prayers. Each day was divided into these eight **sacred** or divine offices.

The times of these prayers were called by the following names: Matins, Lauds, Prime, Sext, Nones, Terce, Vespers and Compline: The first office, 'Matins', began at 2 am and the next seven followed at regular intervals, ending in 'Vespers' in the late afternoon and 'Compline' before the monks or nuns went to sleep at night.

1 Draw a circle like a clock. Fill in the information about the prayer times and work times that you read about in this chapter.

2 Now draw another circle and fill in your daily routines. Compare the daily routines.

KEY TERMS

prayer
Gebet

psalm
Psalm

hymn
Kirchenlied

recite
rezitieren, vortragen

sacred
heilig

cease: aufhören, enden | Matins: Matutin | Lauds: Laudes | Prime: Prim | Terce: Terz | Sext: Sext | Vespers: Vesper | Compline: Komplet

Any work was immediately ceased at these times of daily prayer, often a bell was rang.

Matins: *the night office at 2 am*

lauds: *the early morning service at about 5 am*

Prime: *the 6 am service*

Terce: *Divine office recited at 8–9 am*

Sext: *lunchtime prayers at noon*

Nones: *recited at 3 pm*

Vespers: *the evening service of Divine Office, recited before dark at 4–5 pm*

Compline: *the last of the day services of Divine Office, recited before going to bed (6-7 pm)*

Daily Life – Only study, work and prayer?

Monks ploughing the land with oxen, Germany 1872. This work might have looked very much the same in the Middle Ages.

KEY TERMS

chore
Pflicht

community
Gemeinschaft

illuminated manuscript
ein von Hand geschriebenes, mit Zeichnungen, Illustrationen und Verzierungen, kunstvoll gemalten Großbuchstaben versehenes Manuskript

manual: mit der Hand | labour: Arbeit | property: Eigentum | entangled: verwickelt | weave: weben | embroidery: sticken | to share: teilen

Between prayers monks and nuns were required to perform manual labour. Daily tasks and meals often took place in silence. The lives of medieval monks and nuns were filled with the following work and **chores**:

- washing for the monastery
- working in the garden
- growing the necessary supplies of vegetables and grain
- producing wine, ale, jam and honey
- providing medical care for the **community**
- providing education for novices
- spinning, weaving and embroidery
- **illuminating manuscripts**
- repairing
- cleaning
- copying texts and music
- serving meals
- looking after guests
- looking after sick people
- …

Usually the monks and nuns would shared the work and rotated the different chores. But some jobs needed a specialist's knowledge and were done by trained people. These tasks were often handed over for a lifetime.

1 If you had to choose a chore in a monastery/nunnery, which would you have taken back then? Say why.

Medieval monks and nuns chose to renounce all worldly life and goods and spend their lives working under the strict routine and discipline of life in a medieval monastery or convent. Consequently, medieval monastic life was dedicated to worship, reading, and working. In addition to attending church, the monks and nuns spent many hours in private prayer and meditation.

> The youthful monk is bidden to wash his hands before his meals … He is not to seize upon the vegetables; nor to use his own spoon in the common dish; nor to lean upon the table; nor to cut or dirty the table cloth.

From the Babees Book for the instruction of novices at Barnwell, Source: Brian Williams, Medieval England, Andover 2007, p. 25.

2 Discuss in class, perhaps in a fishbowl: How hard was it to be a monk or a nun?

3 What are your rules at home? Make a list. Show it to your parents and see if they agree.

4 After reading the texts how would you answer the question: Did life at a monastery only mean study, work and prayer? Justify your answer.

Responsibilities of medieval monasteries and convents: social work and science

1 Read the text passages and find a heading for each paragraph. Start like this:

> A medieval monastery performed many works of charity: feeding the hungry, healing sick people and handing out their medicines.

A heading here could be: *works of charity*.

A
A medieval monastery provided education for boys who wished to become priests and those who intended to lead active lives in the world. Young monks learned to read and write, to sing, to read music, and to use Latin.

B
Between prayers, the monks read or copied religious texts and music. Monks were often well educated and devoted their lives to writing and learning. Throughout medieval times the monasteries were practically the only places for **scholarship** and learning. The monks were by far the best-educated members of society. The monks helped peasants to write their wills.

C
A medieval monastery kept **records** of the most important events of their time. Monks and nuns wrote down stories they heard and acted as **chroniclers** of the medieval history of the Middle Ages.

D
The monks and nuns knew a lot about healing and medicine. Sick and injured people often came to the convents to get medical help. Medicinal herbs grew in the gardens, and the nuns and monks produced their own medicine.

E
Many monasteries owned a number of farms. The peasants who lived on these farms paid rent to the monastery like they would to a lord.

F
There were rooms for travellers who needed a place to stay for the night. A medieval monastery received pilgrims and travellers at a period when Western Europe had few inns. Pilgrims visited the monasteries. Pilgrimages were an important part of religious life in the Middle Ages. Many people took these journeys to visit holy shrines and cathedrals like Canterbury Cathedral in England, and places in Spain, Jerusalem and Rome.

G
Monks and nuns **baptized** children, wed couples and were also paid for burial ceremonies. It was common for people to give money or land to monks/nuns so that they would pray for them.

H
Convents were meeting-places in the countryside. They were cultural centres, where people could talk and read books.

I
Monasteries and convents acted as libraries for ancient manuscripts, and many monks and nuns were occupied with laboriously copying sacred texts. In a Medieval monastery and convents the manuscripts of classical authors were copied and so valuable books were preserved.

KEY TERMS

scholarship
Wissenschaft

records
Schriftgut/Aufzeichnungen

Chronicler
Chronist

to baptize
taufen

devote: hingeben/widmen | will: Testament | healing: Heilung | herbs: Kräuter | pilgrims: Pilger | pilgrimage: Pilgerreise | inn: Gasthaus/Wirtshaus | journey: Reise | shrine: Schrein | burial: Beerdigung | countryside: ländlicher Umgebung | laboriously: fleißig | sacred: heilig

Some famous nuns and monks

KEY TERMS

scholar
Wissenschaftler/
Wissenschaftlerin

abbess
Äbtissin, Vorsteherin eines
Klosters

bishop
Bischof

sinful
sündig

hermit
Eremit

to worship
preisen/ehren

inspire: anregen/begeistern/
inspirieren | found: gründen
| advice: Rat | cave: Höhle |
farewell: auf Wiedersehen

Several nuns and monks were leading **scholars** of their time, intellectuals, people with new ideas, men and women of great learning. They inspired and influenced others and left valuable pieces of writings.

1 Read the texts and fill in the gaps. Write down the words from the list in the order in which they belong in the texts.

farewell | age | Benedictine | Christ Church | Italy | translations | natural science | history | miniatures | 529 | advice | chapter

Hildegard von Bingen
The German Hildegard von Bingen (1098–1179) lived with a nun from the _1_ of 8. When she was 15, she took the Benedictine vows. Around 1150 she founded the convent of Rubertsberg. She had visions and wrote them down. She also worked on church song texts and was interested in history, _2_ and medicine. She has been very famous ever since. Many churchmen, **abbesses** and **bishops** asked her for _3_ during her life time.

Hildegard of Bingen receiving the Light from Heaven, c. 1151.

St Benedict
St Benedict left his home in central _4_ at an early age and went to Rome to study. He was a very religious person, saw the **sinful** life around him and decided to live as a **hermit** in a cave. Later he lived at Montecassino where others followed him to live a Christian way of life, saying _5_ to a normal life. His rules, that monks should **worship** God and always keep busy, are known as the Benedictine rule, published in _6_.

Saint Benedict of Nursia handing the Rule, regulations governing monastic life and discipline, to a group of monks. From a 12th century manuscript.

Monk Eadwine

Eadwine was a Benedictine monk and a writer at _7_ in Canterbury. He wrote the Eadwine, also called Canterbury, Psalter around 1160. It includes holy days, prayers, and religious texts. One _8_ is about reading someone's palm. The book is richly illuminated with many _9_ and elaborately drawn initials. At the end, there is a picture of the monk who created this work of art.

Monk Eadwine at work on the manuscript, from the middle of the 12th century.

palm: Handfläche | Psalter: Psalter

Venerable Bede

The Venerable Bede, an English _10_ monk, lived in the 7th century between 673–735. He was born in Tyne, England, entered the monastery of Wearmouth when he was 7, became a deacon at Jarrow at the age of 19 and became a priest at 30. He wrote hymns, poems, and books on natural science and religious matters and also worked on _11_ from the bible since he knew Latin, Greek, and Hebrew. He is well-known because of a five volume book called *The ecclesiastical history of the English people* about the _12_ of England in the early Middle Ages.

The Venerable Bede of Jarrow – sharpening his quill. From a manuscript in Engelberg Abbey, Switzerland.

venerable: ehrwürdig | deacon: Diakon | Hebrew: Hebräisch | volume: Band

1 Get together in a group of five. Assign one of the four texts to each of your group members. Copy the placemat on the right in a bigger version into your history folder, read your text and summarize the information in your area. Get back in your group and present your to the right. White you are presenting, the others take notes in their own placemats in their folders.

2 Discuss: Who was the most interesting person to you? Write the name into the square in the middle of your placemat. If you have the chance, use the internet and find out more about the person that you said was most interesting to your group.

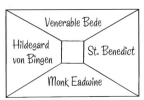

What was the interior of a medieval convent or nunnery like?

the interior: das Innere | purpose: Absicht | quadrangle: viereckiger Innenhof | colonnade: Säulengang | behave: benehmen | storehouse: Speicher | grain: Getreide | dormitory: Schlafsaal | service: Gottesdienst

A medieval convent or nunnery had many different rooms for many different purposes as you will see.

1 Match the description of the room and its name. If you think it is too difficult, use a dictionary. Find the solution sentence. It has five words. Here is some help: MO … AY.

2 Try to find a German name for every room.

3 Quiz a classmate like this: What was the … used for?

M cellarium	
N chapter-house	
S cloister	
U dorter	
S frater	
N garderobe	
C granary	
N infirmary	
E kitchen	
T lavatorium	
E misericord	
I night stair	
T scriptorium	
O warming-house	
A refectory	

N a covered walkway in a convent or nunnery often situated around a quadrangle, often comprised of a plain wall or colonnade on the outer side and a series of windows on the inner side

S contained a trough with running water where nuns washed (lavare in Latin).

V housed the nuns who were too sick or old to take part in the normal monastic life.

X the part of a convent where nuns were disciplined after they had behaved badly.

D a toilet and bathroom in a medieval building

D The only room in a convent, apart from the infirmary and kitchen, where a fire was allowed, also called a calefactory.

O storehouse for grain

K a room in which nuns met daily to hear a chapter of the monastic rule

O store-house of a convent or nunnery

Y the dining hall of a convent or nunnery

N a dormitory. Sometimes the nuns slept in isolated rooms called cells on mattresses stuffed with straw.

S A staircase used by the nuns to enter a church directly from their dormitory in order to attend late night and early morning services.

T the room in a convent used for illuminating or copying manuscripts, which was the scribes' job.

N where food was prepared and cooked.

A another term for a refectory

Walking around a monastery

Here is a plan of the monastery at **St Gall**. This is the earliest **preserved** plan of a monastic building. It was designed in the 9th century and had been kept in the library of the monastery.

1 Look at the **building plan** and complete the names of the rooms. Make a list of all the rooms. You can get help from the table on page 60 (see the green list).

2 Imagine the guests and **visitors** at a convent could not read. Draw an **entry sign** like the one on the right for three rooms.

3 Walking around the monastery: Sit opposite to a partner. Each of you has St Gall's plan in front of you. One of you tells the other in which room you start walking around, the others follows your description with the finger in the plan.
Say: I start at/in ..., I go right/left ..., I turn around ... Then I am there.
Your partner tells you where you stopped walking.

4 What do the rooms tell you about jobs and daily life at a monastery/nunnery?

KEY TERMS

St Gall
Sankt Gallen

to preserve
erhalten

building plan
Gebäudeplan

visitors
Besucher

entry sign
Eintrittsschild

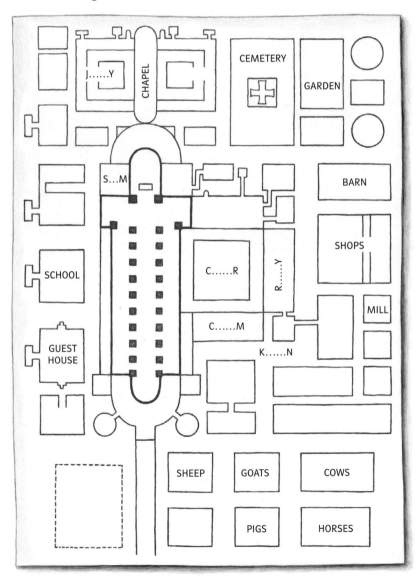

Building plan of St Gall monastery.

What do monasteries and nunneries look like today?

KEY TERMS

Cistercian
Zisterzienser

Benedictine
Benediktiner

Cluniac
Kluniazenser

column: Säule | rotunda: Kuppel | roof: Dach | tower: Turm | nave: Kirchenschiff | bell tower: Glockenturm | wall: Mauer | entry: Durchgang | Monastic orders: Mönchsorden

*The ruins of Fountains Abbey – One of the most famous **Cistercian** monasteries was founded in 1132.*

United Kingdom. Canterbury Cathedral. The Cathedral was a community of Benedictine monks. The Benedictines followed St Benedict´s rule for life which told them to work and pray.

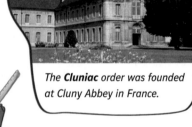

*The **Cluniac** order was founded at Cluny Abbey in France.*

1 Take a look at the pictures and describe the similarities and differences between the monasteries. Write down three sentences.

2 Search in books, travel guides or the internet and bring two pictures of monasteries or convents in England, Germany or Europe to class. Or perhaps you took pictures when you visited a monastery or convent on vacation or on a class trip. Present your pictures in front of the class.

3 You are the art student and looked at many pictures and photos of monasteries and convents across Europe. Draw your most interesting monastery or convent.

Check your knowledge

1 Copy the table into your history folder. Check your knowledge and fill in the chart. Tick true or false. Then check your solutions at the bottom of this page. Correct the wrong answers.

True and false statements	True	False	Correction
1. The names of the three vows were obedience, chastity and poverty.	…	…	…
2. Laudatio is one of the prayer times.	…	…	…
3. A monastery was also a hospital.	…	…	…
4. A monk or a nun could work as a teacher.	…	…	…
5. A nun had a husband.	…	…	…
6. Monks and nuns went to prayer eight times a day.	…	…	…
7. Different monastic orders were the Benedictines, the Cistersians and the Frevolontines.	…	…	…
8. Monks and nuns only lived in the Middle Ages.	…	…	…
9. Hildegard von Bingen lived in Canterbury.	…	…	…

Create a leaflet

1 You are a reporter. Search the internet for a monk or a nun who lives today. Send interview questions via a letter or email. You can also arrange an interview on the phone or interview a monk or nun in your city in person. Use questions like: At what age did you enter the monastery or convent? Why did you become a monk or nun? Where is your monastery or convent? What are your daily routines? What are difficult moments? When do you see friends or relatives? What are your jobs/tasks? …
Bring your email/interview to class.

2 Make a leaflet about the nun or monk you interviewed.

ACTIVITY BOX: How to make a leaflet

1 Take a sheet of paper in DinA3-format.

2 Fold it into 3 sections that have the same size.

3 Find a heading for each section.

4 Think about and plan the layout: Don't only use complete sentences, use photos or draw pictures to illustrate your ideas and statements.

5 Use the information you got from your interview.

Solutions for true and false statements (true = t, false = f):
1t, 2f, 3t, 4t, 5f, 6t, 7f, 8f, 9f

Bildquellennachweis